know your
DOMESTIC AND EXOTIC CATS

Earl Schneider, editor

THE PET LIBRARY LTD

THE PET LIBRARY LTD

Sternco ®

The Pet Library Ltd, subsidiary of Sternco Industries, Inc., 600 South Fourth Street, Harrison, N.J. Exclusive Canadian Distributor: Hartz Mountain Pet Supplies Limited, 1125 Talbot Street, St. Thomas, Ontario, Canada.

Exclusive United Kingdom Distributor: The Pet Library (London) Ltd, 30 Borough High Street, London S.E.1.

PRINTED IN THE NETHERLANDS

1 2 3 4 5 6 7 8 9 10
ISBN 0-87826-602-X

CONTENTS

This Persian and the Margay are companions.

1 A world of choice

Would you like a pet without a tail? Or one with back legs longer than those in front? How about one with hair so curly it looks like a wig? What color do you prefer? We have them in blue, orange, and calico. Or perhaps you'd rather have one so majestic that you'll feel like a royal slave.

Abyssinian kitten.

A lovelier litter of cream Persians would be hard to find.

A Leopard at home.

SALLY ANNE THOMPSON

Whatever your preference in pets, you have no need to look further than *Felis domestica*—the Cat Family!

Yes, this small book is about to sing the cat's praises. And why not? He has been man's friend for over four thousand years. But unlike all the other domesticated animals—dogs, cows, horses, sheep, even elephants—he has never done a lick of work. You say he catches rats? Of course. But he does that for his own pleasure. What is the uncanny hold this little creature has placed on mankind and kept there for so long without ever relaxing his grip?

Even today, in this age of science, he's still a mystery: we still don't know where his purr comes from.

Mohammed cut off the sleeve of his robe rather than disturb his favorite cat, Muessa.

Eli Whitney got the idea for the cotton gin from observing a cat chasing a chicken.

Benjamin West, the famous artist, plucked his first paint brush from puss's tail.

In the fifteenth century English earls wore cloaks trimmed with catskin as a mark of high rank. Visitors to their homes were expected to kiss the family cat.

A cat named Buster who lived in Boston was left $100,000 when his owner died.

Ask any farmer. He'll tell you a cat is worth $50 a year for the protection he gives food storage bins.

And so it goes . . . in history, literature, science, agriculture, art, the cat has played his part.

Now let's see what part he can play for you.

2 Ancient history

The time of the cat's first domestication is lost in the mists of the dawn of history. We have no factual knowledge of its origin. Just theories and legends.

Our favorite legend is the Arabian one: Noah was having a great deal of trouble on the ark. Rats and mice were multiplying rapidly. They were overrunning the ark. Something had to be done. Noah and his sons tried to trap them but failed. They were desperate. Thereupon the lioness sneezed violently and produced the first cat.

While pre-historic man had a dog to share his cave and fire, there is no record that he ever had a cat. Our earliest knowledge of the cat as a domestic animal (rather than a wild beast) comes from Egypt. It is more likely that it was domesticated elsewhere at about the same time, but we have only the ancient Egyptian records to go by. We do know that in about 3500 BC the cat's palmy days began. It was then he became a god and was worshipped. Before then he'd been regarded as a working animal, patrolling the vast granaries for rats and mice. Remember, in those days Egypt was the "breadbasket" of the world.

The seafaring Phoenicians, despite Egyptian laws forbidding the export of cats, smuggled them aboard their grain ships and traded them in lands up and down the Mediterranean; and eventually, interbreeding with native wild cats, the cat spread all over Europe and Asia, taking on his slightly varied forms.

It is interesting to note, however, just how few these slightly varied forms are. Our modern cat closely resembles the mummies of the sacred cats of Egypt who existed long before Moses led the Children of Israel out of bondage.

Unlike the dog, who has been bred and crossbred and inter-

Domestic Short-Hair.

bred into all manner of weird shapes, colors and sizes, from the tiny Mexican Hairless to the huge St Bernard, the cat has changed very little over the centuries, and exists today in only three distinct classifications. These are (1) Long-Haired, formerly Persian and Angora; (2) Domestic and British Short-Haired; and (3) Foreign Short-Haired which includes

Blue-point Siamese kitten.

Manx, Abyssinian, Burmese, Russian Blue, and Siamese cats.

Breeders have discovered that if any pedigreed cat is crossbred with "a common short-hair" for only two generations, all the carefully inbred traits like blue eyes and long fur will quickly disappear, and they'll be back right where the Egyptians started with "just plain cats".

3   Domestic cats

The Domestic Short-Hair

History: The American Domestic Short-Hair has suffered a great deal of injustice by becoming identified as the common "alley cat". In reality, he is just as much of a purebred as are his Persian and Siamese cousins. In fact, he came to this country long before they did. His ancestors *did* come over on the *Mayflower*. The Puritan women took their cats to church with them to keep them warm. But because he bred so freely, his numbers grew until many of his descendants were forced to take to the streets and wilds in order to survive.

Description: Here is a summary of the standards for the Domestic Short-Hair set up by the Cat Fanciers' Association:
Head: Broad with the cheeks especially well-developed in the male. Nose and face medium short with eyes set wide apart. Muzzle should look squarish but should not be as short as the Long-Hairs.
Ears: Medium in size, rounded at the tips, wide-set and not too large at the base.
Eyes: Round, full, set to show breadth of nose.
Chin: Well-developed to form a perpendicular line with the neck.
Neck: Medium short denoting strength, and in proportion to body.
Body: Well-knit and powerful, showing good body depth and full chest.
Tail: Slightly heavy at base tapering to an abrupt end, and in proportion to the body.
Legs and feet: Legs of good substance and in proportion to the body. Not too high on legs. Feet neat and well-rounded.

Coat: Short, thick, even in texture, well-bodied, giving a general appearance of shortness. Somewhat heavier and thicker during winter.

Color: Same as those listed for Long-Hairs.

Condition: Hard and muscular, giving the appearance of strength and vigor.

Balance: All physical aspects should complement one another to present a perfect picture.

Undesirable traits: Too high on legs, receding chin, snub nose, Pekingese-like face, too fine or too fluffy a coat. Long nose or wedge-shaped head, long pointed ears or set too close, narrow slanting eyes or oriental look, neck either too short and thick or too long and slender. Tail too short, or whip-like. Not to resemble the Siamese in any manner.

Remember that a stray cat, wandering the streets, living in alleys, may be a purebred Domestic Short-Hair and a potential cat show winner. So don't turn up your nose the next time someone offers to give you an "alley cat".

British Short-Hair

History: The history of the British Short-Hair is much the same as that of our Domestic—it's just that the Britisher stayed in England. In the United States they are not recognized as a separate breed, and are shown in competition in the same class as our Domestic Short-Hairs.

Description: The British designate their Short-Hairs by color: the British Blue Short-Hair, the British Cream Short-Hair, etc. The coat is plushier than our Short-Hair's and lies close to a body which is powerfully built with a thick chest. The head is round, and the eyes large and full. For the Blue there must be absolutely no markings or shading and the coat should be a medium blue all over. The eyes must be copper or

A rare Lynx-point Siamese.

orange. For the Cream there must be a level cream color with no white anywhere. Eyes must be copper or hazel. The Blue Cream is a mixture of the two colors with no patches of either color. Eyes the same as Cream.

Cream Persian. A solid color like this is called a "self color".

Characteristics: These cats have the same natures as our Domestics, and they are just as beautiful. However, not too many of them are in this country.

Siamese

History: When most people think of exotic cats they think of the Siamese. These beautiful animals are among the most prized of all cats. It is generally believed that they originated in the country of Siam—modern-day Thailand. Siamese cats were considered both royal and sacred. They helped the soldiers to guard the king's palace. They first appeared in the Western World in 1884 when a British emissary to Siam returned with a pair of them. Their names were Pho and Mia and their children carried off first prizes at the Crystal Palace Exhibition.

Description: If you want a cross-eyed cat you will have a hard time finding it among the Siamese of today. When they first became popular here, crossed-eyes, a kink in the tail, and a large heavy body were the distinctive marks of the breed. Over the years, however, most of these traits have been bred out. Your Siamese will now be a sleek, trim animal. But he will have the deep blue eyes of the original Siamese and the same distinctive markings or "points" as they are called. These are the ears, mask, tail and feet, and they will be of the same color as the body but in a much deeper shade. For example, the Seal-point has a tan body with dark brown points; the Blue-point has a bluish-gray body with dark blue points. Siamese kittens are almost white when they are born and without their famous points. These develop as the kitten grows. The Siamese head is long and tapered. His ears are large and pricked. His coat is finely textured, short and glossy.

The points of the Siamese are divided for show into four classifications. They are: Seal-point, Blue-point, Chocolate-point, and Lilac-point. In recent years other colors known as Frost-point, Red-point, and Lynx-point have been developed. Undoubtedly there will be others coming along.

Charateristics: In many behavioral respects the Siamese has doglike qualities. You may find them demanding, however, as Siamese are noted for their rather loud voices. All in all though, they are among the most lovable of pets and can be purchased at reasonable prices.

Persian and Angora (Long-Hairs)

History: Today there are no purebred Angora cats to be found in this country. Frequently a cat sold as an Angora is merely a half-breed Persian. They have disappeared because Long-haired cat breeders interbred the two strains until the Persian charateristics dominated.

Description: Here is, most fanciers believe, the most beautiful of all the cats. His round head and powerfully built body make his bearing royal. His face should be flat or pushed in like a Pekingese dog's. The ears should be tufted. The legs short and stout making the body appear close to the ground. Eye color varies with coat color.

Color: Long-haired cats are bred and judged for both color and coat. The great variety of colors offers you a wide choice.

Black: The coat is jet black from the root to the tip of each hair. Eye color may be copper or orange. He should be groomed frequently to maintain the coat's glossy sheen. In old age the cat must be kept healthy to maintain this gloss.

White: A clean and beautifully-groomed long-haired white is a sight to behold. The two varieties are determined by eye color. The orange-eyed is the result of breeding a white with a blue, a cream, or even a black. Blue-eyed cats are maintained by breeding whites. For showing, the white must be absolutely pure in color with no black hairs or yellow tinges.

Cream: The color of cream all the way down to the roots of

This is a tricolor Persian. Tricolor is sex linked, all cats of this color are female.

his long hair. The underparts must be no paler and the eyes should be a deep copper.

Blue: This magnificent animal is the product of a cross of a pure white and a pure black. The earliest blues were some-

Lilac-point Siamese.

what darker than those preferred today, but all shades are still allowed in shows. The coat, however, must be of an even color throughout. Deep copper or orange eyes are desired.

Orange or Red: These cats are popular not only for their

unusual color but also because they are valuable to use in breeding other colors. The deep red is rarely seen as even cats that are shown sometimes have some tabby markings. Again the eyes should be copper.

Smokes: Here is one of the most striking of the Long-Hairs. The color is the result of a light undercoat, as nearly white as possible, that is tipped with black. The head and face should be completely black and set off by a pale ruff. A blue may be used to make the tipping a light blue shade. The round head and deep orange or copper eyes accentuate the mask-like beauty.

Tabbies: All tabbies should have the same markings. There should be swirls on the cheeks and the "M" on the forehead, two chest stripes, solid stripes on the sides, leg stripes, and tail rings. In the brown tabby, the ground color is sable and the markings are black with hazel or copper eyes. The red tabby has a coat of deep red but markings of an even darker red. The undercarriage must be the same color. Their eyes are orange or copper. The silver tabby ground color is pure silver. Its markings should be dense black. The eyes are hazel or green.

It is important that in all tabbies the markings should be distinct and not mottled or brindled.

Chinchilla: These cats have a ticked coat. The undercoat is pure white and the end of each hair is tipped black. The effect is a silver or lavender shading. The eyes may be blue-green or deep emerald green.

Other colors: An almost endless variety may be produced by interbreeding these colors. And, occasionally, a proud breeder can display a beautiful cat whose unusual color resulted accidentally or so it would seem.

Characteristics: Many people consider the Persian a poor pet because they have heard that he is "too aloof". The opposite is nearer the truth. They are extremely affectionate cats.

Maine Coon Cat

Although this prolific and beautiful cat is not recognized as a special breed, he exists in New England, chiefly in the states of Maine and Massachusetts. He is a true Domestic Long-Hair but how his ancestors arrived in New England is clouded in legend. Some claim he is half cat, half raccoon. Even more colorful is the claim that he was brought to Maine by royal refugees fleeing the French Revolution. The truth, most likely, is a little more prosaic. He was brought home from Angora, Turkey, by sailors in the days of the sailing ships when Yankee Clippers spanned the world, and is now a cross between the Angora and Domestic Short-Hair.

Manx

History: The name comes from the Isle of Man in the Irish Sea, where the cat is still bred. Many owners believe that his ancestors swam ashore from sinking Spanish ships during the wars between England and Spain. The historians trace the Manx much farther away to the Malayan Peninsula.

Description: The most distinctive feature of the Manx, and it comes instantly to mind when the breed is mentioned, is his complete lack of tail, not even a stub. In fact, there's a dimple where the tail should be. Another distinctive feature is its luxurious double coat. The undercoat is fine and soft. Over this is a second coat of longer and coarser hair. Another way to distinguish a Manx is by his peculiar build. His hindquarters are higher than his shoulders and when he walks he appears to be hopping or at times walking downhill. The Manx comes in all colors and all colors are acceptable for showing. Their heads should be round and cheeky.

Abyssinian.

Characteristics: The Manx is disappearing. They are difficult to breed and often when tailless cats are bred with other tailless cats, the kittens are very weak. If you are lucky enough to have a Manx, you have a faithful pet who is intelligent and a good ratter, and very attached to his master.

Infant Bobcats are appealing creatures.

Abyssinian

History: The Abyssinian is much like the European wild cat except, of course, for his gentleness which verges on timidity. The Abyssinians are comparatively new in this country, the first ones having been brought here in the 1930's. There are some who believe that these are the direct descendants of the cats worshipped in Egypt thousands of years ago.

Description: The striking feature is its color. Most preferred is a ruddy brown or brick tone. This is difficult to achieve because each hair in the coat of the Abyssinian is ticked or banded by three different colors. If the brick color is the largest of the bands, then the wanted color results. The nose is brick red. The "Abby" is of medium size and, like the Siamese, has an oriental bone structure. Standing, they sometimes appear to be on tiptoe. The head is not as wedge-shaped as the Siamese and it flows into the arched neck. The eyes are almond-shaped. They may be gold, green, or hazel.

Characteristics: He prefers to purr rather than meow and this makes him a little special. An active cat, he loves to play in water. Related to this is his constant concern with personal cleanliness. Unfortunately, for many would-be owners, he is still an expensive cat to buy in this country.

Burmese

History: His history is little known; even his country of origin has not been proven. A female was brought into the United States in the 1930's and, apparently, most of our present Burmese are descended from her. And for once the American breeders got ahead of the English. The Burmese was bred in this country before he was known in England.

Description: The true Burmese is not an oriental. Instead of the wedge-shaped head of the Siamese, the Burmese head is round. His eyes are round. His body is muscular and thick rather than lithe and slim. The legs are proportioned to the body and the feet are round. The tail is of medium length and slightly tapered. The fine-textured hair is a solid sable brown all over. And the golden eyes add the finishing touch to one of nature's loveliest color schemes.

Characteristics: Although dignified in manner, he makes a most affectionate pet. And he seems to be as considerate of you as you should be of him. Like the Abyssinian, however, he is very expensive to purchase.

Russian Blue (Maltese)

History: The origin of the Russian Blue is obscure in spite of all the legends that it was once the Palace cat of the Czars. It is, in all likelihood, just a sport of one of the Foreign Short-Hairs. I have seen a Domestic Short-Hair whose mother was part Siamese; the build and color of this mixed breed were very like a Russian Blue's. However, darker markings and the wrong eye-color distinguished her from the true Russian Blue. It is curious but true that once in a long while a Russian Blue will turn up in the litter of an "everyday" cat. So, if this happens to you, consider yourself fortunate, but don't go around proclaiming that his aristocratic ancestors escaped the Russian Revolution. Call him a Maltese, or an American Blue if you want to be patriotic.

Description: The head is triangular like that of the Siamese. The body is lithe and slender. It is the essence of feline in its appearance. The short close-lying coat has a distinct sheen. In texture it is like mink. The color is a medium to dark shade of blue, solid without shading, and free of any markings. The emerald green eyes, set wide apart, are almond-shaped. *Faults:* White or tabby markings, cobby or heavy build, or square head.

Characteristics: To sum up, the Russian Blue resembles the Siamese more than any other breed; the obvious difference being its solid blue coat. A perfect Russian Blue is hard to come by because it takes from one to two years for the kitten to develop the correct coat-color and silkiness, and its eyes remain yellow for about that same length of time.

Rex

History: Here is a newcomer to the cat family. Strangely enough, the Rex is not the product of scientific breeding but

Burmese.

a natural mutation of the Domestic Short-Hair. The first known Rex did not appear until 1950 and the breed has been developed only since then.

Description: He is called "Rex" because of his curly hair which resembles the "Rex" wig worn by English judges and

The king of beasts is a cat.

attorneys. The wavy hair seems to suggest that the cat has just come back from the hairdresser's. The coat appears on long slender bodies. A Siamese with the curly Rex coat is a truly unusual animal. As with the Manx, almost any color is permissible. The hips are heavy in proportion to the body; the head while not too long is longer than it is wide. The long and slender tail is sometimes tufted and forms an amusing counterpart to his curled whiskers. The medium-sized eyes are deep-set, oval, and their color varies with the coat color.

Characteristics: An intelligent, affectionate, and "very special" pet. He is becoming more and more popular and your chances of acquiring one increase daily.

4 Jungle cats

Ocelots and Margays

History: These are true jungle cats, and if you are thinking of buying one, first consider the special problems that they present. Unlike the other cats mentioned in this booklet, Margays and Ocelots are not bred in captivity; they are captured wild on the plains and in the forests. They can be purchased at some of the big city pet shops, but you will most likely have to put in an order for one and wait some time for its delivery.

Description: The ground color of these cats ranges from yellow or even off-white through the darker toast and rust colors. Spots, stripes, bars, or freckles in varying patterns form the markings. A mature Ocelot can grow to four feet and weigh over 70 pounds, but the average is three feet and 25 pounds. The Margay is smaller. Some of them weigh as little as six pounds, and the largest weighs no more than 20. The Ocelot's tail is shorter and more "club-shaped" than the Margay's, and its legs are heavily muscled. The head of the Ocelot is quite broad and less wedge-shaped than the Margay's. When they are very young, even experienced dealers cannot always tell them apart. But if you are about to purchase one it is important to know what you are getting because of the grown cat's eventual size and strength.

Characteristics: Before buying an Ocelot or Margay, or any other jungle cat, give serious thought to the many problems, expenses, and changes in your way of life that such a pet will demand. In many communities, ownership is prohibited by law. Keeping one as a pet presents a challenge. Not only

SI MERRILL

This Margay enjoys sleeping with his owner.

do they eat more than the domestic cat, they need more room to roam. They cannot be kept in cages except at night. They must be tamed after purchase. Some of them take to domestic ways and become true pets. Others, however, revert in later life to their jungle characteristics. The tamed ones do make striking pets!

An adult Puma or Mountain Lion.

The large prominent eyes show that the Margay is nocturnal.

Another volume in the Pet Library series, *Know your Ocelots and Margays (No. 756)*, discusses in great detail the specialized care that these exotic cats demand.

Other jungle cats

The statement made about Ocelots and Margays applies equally, if not more so, to these three "cats".

Cheetah: This is the largest of the wild cats. He can be trained to run down game and has been used as a hunter for centuries. About the size of the leopard, he can be tamed if captured when very young. A Cheetah in today's market costs about $3500, so because of this, his size, and his wild strength, I do not believe too many readers will want one.

Jaguarundi: The Jaguarundi is found from Argentina to Texas and lives on small animals and frogs. He is three or four feet long but almost half of his length is tail. He is short-legged and usually dark brown in color.

Serval: These cats, smaller than Margays, are sometimes seen in pet shops. They are Old World animals, not native to the Americas.

5 Getting your cat

So you've decided you want an exotic cat. Where do you get one? Not too many people are giving them away free these days. Start with the yellow pages of the phone book. Look under "Cats" and "Pet Shops", or in smaller directories under "Dogs and Other Pets". Look too in the classified columns of your local newspapers. In large cities, exotic kittens are not hard to find; in smaller communities you may have to write one of the four cat associations for addresses of nearby breeders. They are:

Cat Fanciers' Association, Inc.,
20615 Patton Court, Detroit, Michigan;

American Cat Fanciers' Association,
1104 Bouldin Blvd., Austin, Texas;

The American Cat Association,
Lakeside, Barren County, Michigan;

The United Cat Federation, Inc.,
3517 South Pacific, San Pedro, California.

There is also a magazine for cat fanciers which has a classified-ad section advertising pedigreed kittens for sale. It is

Cats Magazine,
4 Smithfield St., Pittsburgh 22, Pa.

Exotic kittens are usually sold in two categories, and in two price ranges: Kittens sold as pets only—they are purebred but less than perfect in prizewinning features. You can buy one of these for from $25 to $100. Kittens in the second category are ones that represent their particular breed so well that they can compete in pet shows and be used for breeding more ribbon winners. Their prices vary according to their individual pedigree but they are, of course, much more expensive than those in the first category.

Choosing your kitten

Never buy a kitten less than seven weeks old. To be in the best of health, they should remain with their mothers until that age; they should not be fully weaned until they are eight

Baby Serval.

A baby Ocelot.

Adam Pressman and a baby Jaguar.

weeks old. An indication that they are old enough to be taken away from their mother is their sharp white teeth—two full rows of them.

Avoid kittens that are listless, weak-legged, or have runny eyes. Beware of a bloated belly; this can indicate worms. A protruding spine could be a sign of undernourishment. Wave a piece of string in front of the kitten. Do its bright eyes react? Make a sharp noise behind it. Is its hearing okay? Check on fleas, ticks, or a strong odor. Is the establishment itself clean? Do all their other pets for sale look healthy?

Check on the kitten's inoculation certificate. He should by now have had at least one vaccination for feline enteritis, a malignant cat disease, and preferably two, since a booster shot is also needed.

If you are paying for a purebred cat, check its pedigree. However, the seller should give you more than just the pedigree. If he hasn't already registered your choice with one of the Cat Associations, he should instruct you how to do it; and, even if it has been registered, you will have to file for a change of ownership.

Male or female?

Which to choose? Cats each have their own personality. That is why it is difficult to generalize about males being more active than females, or females being more docile than males. Each will develop his or her own individuality and will be much more affected by his or her new family environment than by sex. Obviously, if you're buying a pedigreed cat for breeding purposes, you'll want the female; making money by breeding a Tom is a limited field and you miss all the fun of raising the litter.

If your pedigreed kitten is to be just a pet, most breeders urge that you have it neutered. Unaltered males often soil sofas and rugs and leave a strong smell; unaltered females when in "heat" several times a year become noisy and restless and try to get out of the house to search for a stray Tom.

A female should not be spayed before her first heat, which usually occurs in her seventh or eighth month. It can happen earlier, but if you delay, don't worry. The operation can be performed at any age. The male is usually neutered when about nine months old but he too can wait until later.

Baby Tiger—cute as cubs, they are certainly not recommended as household pets.

STANLEY PRESSMAN

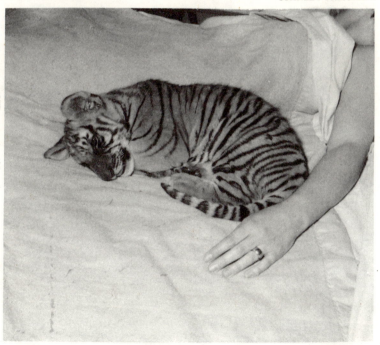

6 General care

Diet

So, you buy a kitten two months old, or older. Ask its previous owner about its diet. Then try to duplicate this (even to brand names, if possible) for the first few days until the kitten adjusts to its new home. You'll find that the new member of your family has a huge appetite but a small capacity. That's all to the good. His stomach should be kept round and full. Feed often, but keep the food fresh. Discard leftovers. Give him four meals a day, about four hours apart. After he's four months old, you can reduce them to three a day, and when he's a young adult of eight months, two or even one a day will be enough. At each feeding, give him as much as he will eat. Rarely will a cat overeat.

Commercially prepared kitten food plus Pablum and milk is standard fare. Baby food (the kind that comes in small jars) is a good alternative. Evaporated milk can be used. See that there is always fresh water in the bowl, but do not replenish it by adding more water. Dump out the stale and refill. Feeding dishes should be kept scrupulously clean; never let uneaten food remain exposed. Wrap it in a plastic bag and return it to the refrigerator for the next feeding. Never feed a kitten, or even a mature cat, food right out of the refregerator. Warm it first, either by letting hot water run over it, or letting it sit for awhile before feeding.

After your kitten is four months old, a hunk of meat can be added to its diet. Offer it chunk-style: too big to gulp and swallow, but big enough to chew. See that it gets cod-liver oil regularly. Cats are prone to hair-balls—Long-Hairs more so than Short-Hairs. When cats preen themselves they ingest their own fur. A regular dose, say once a week, of mineral oil, will help them rid their digestive track of swallowed hair. Cat kibble or even dog meal can be mixed with any food you offer. Vitamins and food supplements especially prepared for cats are available at pet counters. Use according to the package's directions. Some cats refuse food that has any supplement added. In this case, feed them with an eyedropper.

Some cats enjoy greens and other vegetables along with their meat diet. You may learn this by accident after yours has chewed on your favorite house plant. Try him on beans, carrots, spinach, or other non-starchy vegetables.

Milk is a necessity for young kittens but not for mature cats. Too much milk can increase their calcium intake and cause urinary stones. If your cat does enjoy milk (many do not) be sure that it is not left out of the refrigerator long enough to spoil. In a spoiled state, milk can be a too-powerful laxative.

Housebreaking

Here you are in luck. The average kitten requires almost no housebreaking because his mother has already done it for you. Just give him a good-sized plastic or enamel litter box (easily washable) big enough for him to turn around in, remembering, of course, that he's going to grow. There are on the market and easily available at groceries and super-markets as well as pet shops various types of "kitty litter" which absorb both moisture and odor. You will find this sort of filler much better than dirt or sand.

Keep the litter box in one place (there is no reason why you can't have more than one box—indoors and out if you prefer) and make sure that your kitten knows where it is. When he first arrives, take him to it, sit him down in it, and then scratch the litter with his paws. If he does seem slow in catching on, leave some of his droppings in the box for a reminder.

A cat scratching station will help satisfy his urge to scratch.

Obviously it is up to you to keep the litter box clean. The solid wastes should be removed daily (a small garden trowel is good for this) and flushed down the toilet. The moistened litter should be stirred up from the bottom of the box, and more litter added. The box itself should be washed and sterilized regularly.

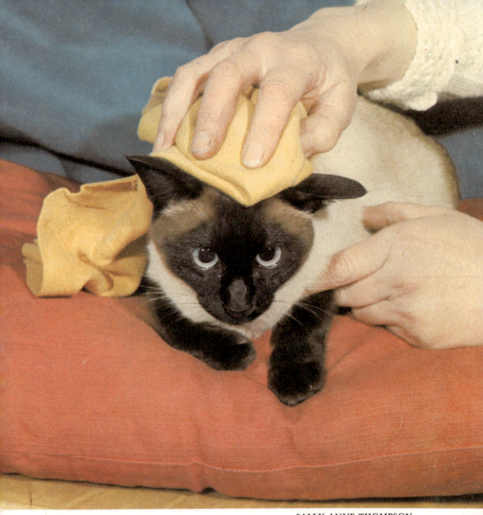

A good rubdown with a rough cloth will help cleanse your cat's coat and keep it shiny.

The bed

Excellent wicker, plastic and wooden beds are available, but a cardboard carton will do in an emergency. Make sure it's kept out of drafts in a warm spot. Once your kitten gets a bit older, he'll improvise a bed for himself wherever he sees fit.

Give him a warm pad to sleep on. High-sided boxes seem to give him a better sense of security. Some of the store-bought beds even have covers or tops.

Now let's see: what else do you need for the new arrival? Toys? Have a few waiting for him. Rubber ones that squeak or make some kind of noise are favorites. Crazy rolling balls as well as balls attached to elastic cords will delight him no end.

Catnip is a kind of mint that almost all cats love. To them, it's more than just a flavor, it's an intoxicating thing. A pinch of catnip will be rolled on, tossed, rubbed and pawed until you take it away. Many toys are impregnated with the aroma. There is such a thing as too much catnip, so use it for just an occasional treat.

Grooming

Brushing: Obviously, Short-Hairs need less brushing than Long-Hairs. But it is a good practice to brush any cat regularly. A long-haired cat must be brushed every day; a Short-Hair every few days. The earlier you begin brushing the better; this way, your cat will learn to enjoy the brushing rather than fight it. There are various kinds of brushes on the market; I suggest you let your pet shop dealer recommend the one that is best for your particular cat. For Long-Hairs, a round-tooth steel comb will also be needed. Gently brush both with and against the "grain" to loosen any dead hair and keep the skin clean and free of scale. With Long-Hairs, you may have to tease out snarls with the end of the comb, always holding the tuft of hair in your fingers so the pull won't be on the skin.

When you've finished brushing a Short-Hair, rub your hands over its body with the grain. Nothing can beat the human hand as a short-haired cat groomer. There is just enough oil in it to produce a silken sheen and, at the same time, cause the hairs to lie close together.

Bathing: Bathe only when absolutely necessary—such as an exploratory venture into a coal bin. Cats do not like deep water nor do they like a temperature much warmer than their own—about 102°F. Use a commercially prepared cat soap or shampoo. Lather the coat well, working it down to the skin. Avoid washing the head. Wipe it off with a damp, unsoaped washcloth. Now rinse thoroughly, several times. It is important that every bit of soap be rinsed away. Dry thoroughly when you are finished, and keep him out of drafts until you are sure that he is dry. Commercially prepared dry shampoos are available at pet shops. Many owners prefer these. Others use oven-dried bran, brushed in and brushed out.

Paws and claws: Check feet for cuts and bruises. If your cat limps, check between the toes for a pebble or splinter. Keep the claws trimmed too. These are just like human nails and can be cut without causing pain. Be careful, however, not to nick the blood vessel which nourishes the claw. If you're attempting the job for the first time, use heavy-bodied nail clippers and with a quick snip just nip off the sharp tips. If the nails have grown too long, better turn the job over to a vet.

Most cats like to scratch and this tendency helps to keep their nails worn down. To protect your furniture, give him a scratching post. All pet departments carry them. Set it up in a permanent spot. He'll spend hours scratching the wood.

Eyes and ears: Wipe mucus from the corner of the eye with a damp cotton swab. If the eyes are irritated, a mild boric solution may be used as a wash. All but the most stubborn conditions can be cleared up by using the commercially pre-

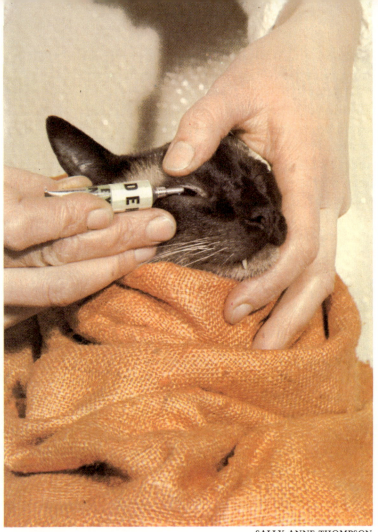

Use eye ointment for infected or watery eyes. To minimize struggling first wrap the cat up well.

pared cat eyewashes available in pet departments. But if the condition persists, it's time for professional assistance. As to ears, wipe away the dirt with a cotton swab dipped in olive oil. Don't dig in any deeper than you can see. If the ears are irritated, medicated ear washes are also available.

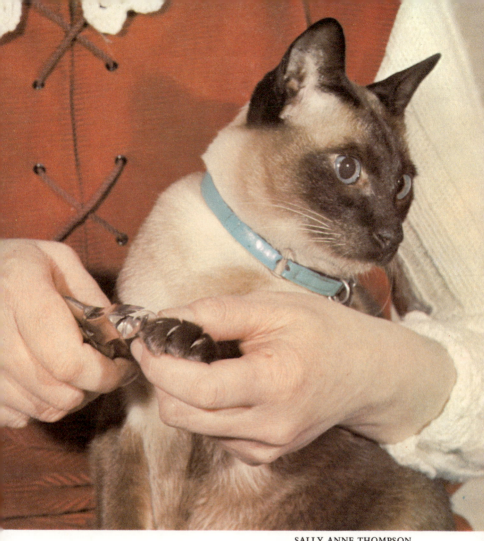

A cat's claws should be trimmed regularly.

Teeth: Tooth decay is common with cats. Diet is the cause. They are fed soft foods endlessly although nature gave them teeth to tear into raw meat. That is why we suggested earlier that you feed meat in chunks. The cat has no way of keeping his teeth clean except by proper diet. A small bone (not fish or chicken) on which there are a few shreds of meat can serve as a "toothbrush"; kibbled food in the diet will also help. Tartar accumulates and must be removed. This means that periodic visits to the vet are in order.

7 Health

A cat is a hardy animal, well equipped to withstand routine drafts and chills. However, being informed about the more usual cat maladies will help you to recognize and treat them. If any minor ailment persists, or if the cat's temperature goes over 102°F. (take rectally) and stays there for 24 hours, it's time to consult your veterinarian. Modern wonder drugs, a bit of care and understanding, can usually put your cat back on his feet in no time.

Hair Balls: When cats preen themselves. loose hair is swallowed and hair balls form in the intestines and cause obstructions. Prevention is easier than cure. Add a little mineral oil or cod-liver oil to the diet once a week. If your cat sits around hunched up, loses his appetite and coat tone, check his temperature. If it is still normal (101 to 102°F.) hair balls should be suspected. If the temperature is above 103°F. call the vet.

Constipation: Diet is often to blame. Hair ball may be the cause. Make sure your cat has good roughage—vegetables and dog meal or biscuits will help. For fast relief, give mineral or cod-liver oil. But remember that a laxative is only an an immediate solution. A proper diet will have to be maintained.

Diarrhea: This can be caused by diet too. More bulk is again the answer. Kaopectate, a teaspoonful every three hours, will often give immediate relief. Diarrhea is a symptom of many diseases so if it doesn't clear up quickly, start looking for other causes.

Pneumonitis: A common cat ailment characterized by frequent sneezing, runny eyes and nose, emaciation, diarrhea, a poor coat, and a tendency of the kitten to cry. Make this test: hold a toy in front of, and level with, the cat's eyes, a few inches away. When you've caught his attention, slowly lift the object so he must raise his head to keep it in view. If his head twitches and jerks instead of rising smoothly, this is a good sign of pneumonitis and a trip to the vet's is in order. If treatment is started early enough, the outlook for recovery is good. A vaccine is also available.

Feline enteritis: The correct name for this virulent cat disease is Panleucopenia. It is sometimes called distemper although it is unrelated to canine distemper. The symptoms are high fever (104°F.), extreme vomiting, and loss of appetite. This last is usually the first sign. Symptoms can develop within a matter of hours and the kitten can be dead within a day or two. This is why inoculations are so important—in fact absolutely necessary. No professed lover of cats will have a kitten that has not been inoculated against Infectious Enteritis. A kitten is given two shots which immunize it for about two years. It should then be given a booster shot. After three years, cats seem to develop a natural immunity to this dread disease. If you acquire an adult cat with no way of knowing whether or not she has been inoculated, have her inoculated to be on the safe side. It can't do her any harm, and it may save her life.

An easy way to administer medicine or oil is to dab a little on his nose. He'll promptly lick it off.

Bronchitis: This is the most common of cat respiratory diseases. Inflammation spreads rapidly through the bronchial tubes into the lungs. Fever, a hacking cough, and listlessness are the most obvious symptoms. Tempt your cat to eat because the nourishment keeps up her strength and makes recovery more rapid. Keep her dry and warm, even to the extent of packing her in hot-water bottles. Moist air is necessary to ease her breathing and loosen the cough; if

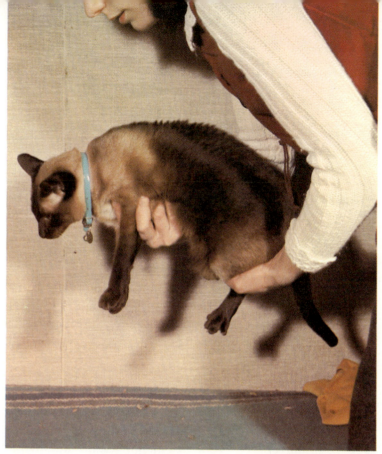

SALLY ANNE THOMPSON
Should it be necessary to lift your cat, support him firmly at both ends.

you have an electric vaporizer, use it; if not, a steam kettle. The vet will prescribe expectorant mixtures and antibiotics.

Worms: All worms are not the same. There are, to name a few, roundworms, tapewroms, hookworms, and threadworms. Each requires its own special treatment. So be sure of your worm and the medication you are using, if you decide to worm the cat yourself. If you don't, take a sample of its stool to the veterinarian for a microscopic examination.

8 Training

Believe it or not cats can be trained. Despite their independent natures they learn that they can please you and gain attention if they obey your wishes. The way to train one is through his stomach. You'll be amazed at the things he can be taught by working through his appetite. A hungry cat will learn fast to get food as a reward. And missing a meal or two won't do him a bit of harm.

Knowing his name

Choose a short name—one that sounds like no other in the household—and use it whenever you address him or call him to be fed. When he responds, reward him with a snack. He will soon associate the two things.

Lead and collar

For no apparent reason, many cat owners do not train their pets to accept a collar and leash. These handsome accessories give you control over your cat in public and add to his safety. Because of the small size and flexibility of most cats' heads, a harness is preferable to a collar. A puppy harness is not suitable for a cat. He needs a special figure-eight harness which he can't slip out of. Let your pet shop dealer show you how to put it on.

Put it on your pet for a few minutes each day while he's still a kitten. Make it playtime with lots of fun. Gradually lengthen the periods during which it is on. Then leave it on all day. Once he's grown accustomed to the harness, tie a rag or bit of clothesline to it—about a foot long. He'll scratch and paw at it and tear it to shreds. Let him. Replace it, or attach the new leash. Let him drag this around for a while—under supervision of course, so the loop can't catch on something and strangle him. As with the harness, gradually extend the periods during which it is worn.

A good place to start training him to walk on leash is in the house. Here there are no unusual noises to frighten him. It is a good idea to let him lead you during the first lessons. He will come to feel that this new idea of yours is not going to restrict him in any way. When you do try to lead him, he will probably pull against the leash. Let him learn that pulling does not pay. He'll catch on quickly that you're in control.

Now you're ready to walk him outside. Be prepared for this, though: until he's learned better, every time he's frightened he'll try to climb your leg and perch on your shoulders. A frightened cat always climbs. You'll quickly discover that a cat does not have the tendency to pull ahead or drag behind that a dog has. Reward him with kind words when he walks close by your side.

It is particularly important to break your cat to the leash if you intend to do any traveling. A cat on a leash is much less likely to become frightened and run away.

House manners

Cats love high places and soft spots in just about equal proportions. Let yours have some leeway around the house, but also let him know what is *verboten*. A stern reprimand like a guttural "Ah-ah" or a sharp "No!" will help him learn. If it doesn't, a fold of newspaper rolled up and taped at the ends, and cracked like a whip on the floor beside him, will reinforce your wishes. Remember, though, that when a chair or sofa is placed off-limits, it must stay that way. You can't expect to relax the rules one time and enforce them the next. Confusion won't train a cat but it will give him a nervous breakdown.

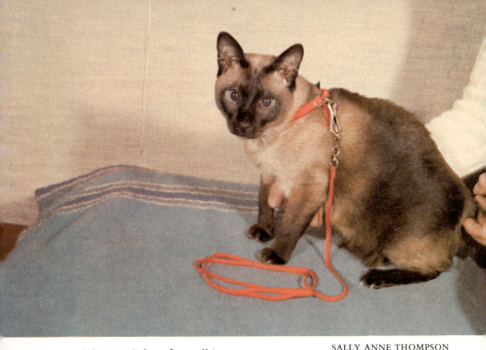

A harness is best for walking a cat.

Most cats are fascinated by a flame. They will sit and stare at it for hours.

Cats are great hunters.

9 Cat shows

We're speaking of official cat shows now, sponsored by the various Cat Associations listed earlier, and not those neighborhoood fun shows where anything goes and all good cats get together.

If you are considering entering your cat in a show, this should govern your choice of pedigreed kitten. But showing goes far beyond pedigree. It entails special diet, grooming to the "nth" degree, and specialized training. The cat must become used to travel, to living in a cage, and to being handled by strangers.

Whether you win or lose shouldn't be important. The feeling of pride you'll get from exhibiting your pet should be what counts. In fact, let me say firmly that if there is any thought in your mind that your cat's losing would alter your affection toward him, forget the whole idea right now.

If not, write one of the Cat Associations for complete details and entry blanks. Their addresses are listed in the first part of this book.

Siamese-point Persian or Himalayan.

10 Breeding

The female comes into heat with the coming of warm weather. Her first heat of the year will usually be in March; then she'll come into heat every month until mid-summer when she should (but may not) have a two or three month respite. She will again have two or three more heats in the fall. Heat periods will be about 29 to 30 days apart, and will last up to 17 days. The acceptance, or optimum mating period of three or four days, occurs midway. She will have her very first heat when she's five or six months old, but she should not be bred before reaching maturity (one year old), and developing a strong body. Be watchful, though, of the queen who has just had a litter. She may be in heat again just a few days after having given birth.

Each queen is an individual: her heat periods will vary from others of the species, so they should be carefully noted and charted if you intend to breed her, and get her to the Tom on time. She should be offered to the male on the second or third day of her optimum period. The best procedure is to shut them up together in a place where they can do no harm, and where she cannot hide. If the time is ripe the queen will accept the Tom readily enough. She should be left with him long enough for several matings to take place—several hours at least, possibly overnight.

The gestation period of the cat is 61 days, but there are some strains and individuals in which the period is as short as 57 days. Since proper timing is of utmost importance so as to be ready for the litter, try to discover how long the gestation periods have been in her pedigree. If you've calculated carefully and her time has gone beyond 64 days, better call the vet.

Speaking of vets, however, let me say here and now that

Solid black kittens are quite rare and in great demand. Most blacks have white hairs on the chest, stomach or paws.

your cat should have her kittens at home; never unless there are highly special reasons should she be sent to an animal hospital. Just as it is with human mothers, this is a difficult time for her and she wants to be with those she loves.

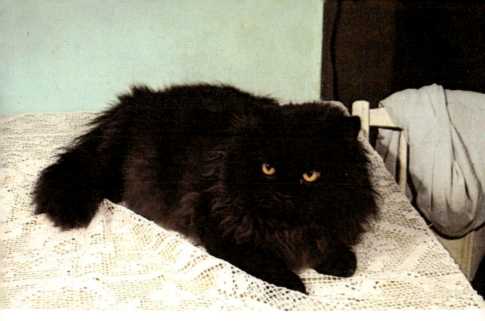

The gleaming orange eyes contrast with the glistening black coat to create a spectacular picture. Truly the black Persian cat, far from being bad luck, is a pleasure to behold. The person who can obtain an all-black Persian like this is very fortunate.

A Black Panther—frequently found in a litter with normal spotted sisters and brothers.

When she is about five weeks pregnant, start giving her more food. Add milk to her diet, as much as she will drink, and give her salad or olive oil every two or three days to prevent constipation.

Now comes the battle of nests: she'll want it one place, you'll want it in another, more practical, area. If at all possible, let her have her way; otherwise she may move the kits from your spot to her own choice soon after they are born. The place chosen should be dry and dimly lit. Place a box there; it should be about 18 inches square with eight inch sides, low enough for the mother to go over, high enough to keep the kits inside.

Spread old terry cloth towels several layers deep over the bottom of the box. Then as each layer becomes soiled it can be removed without too much disturbing the mother and her newborn kits. Never use wool in a nesting box, the kits might eat it.

The mother will start showing signs of nervousness about a day before the kits are due. She may refuse to eat, and will stay close to her chosen nest.

A normal litter usually takes about four hours from first to last kitten. But it varies considerably. Four kits may be born in half an hour, or it may take six hours for them to be delivered. Many times with a cat's first litter there is only one kit. Later there may be as many as eight. Siamese are noted for their large litters.

In the majority of cases, the queen will need no help from you. She will rip open the amniotic sac and sever the umbilical cord herself, cleaning each kit thoroughly. But be ready to help if she needs help. The sac *must* be ripped open or the kit will suffocate, the cord must be cut about one inch from its body. She will probably eat the placenta. There are chemicals in this which start lactation.

If the cat labors too long in delivering her first or her last kit, better call the vet and let him either ease your mind that everything is okay or advise you what to do. On rare occasions, it may be necessary to get a grip with a terry cloth washrag on a half-born kit and pull. Monstrosities are sometimes born. They should, of course, be painlessly destroyed immediately.

The kittens will be born blind, deaf and helpless. Leave them alone with their mother after making sure that they will not be accidentally smothered; that their bedding is clean and dry; that they are in a dimly lit place and no bright light can strike their closed eyes; and that their mother has milk to feed them. Check this by pressing a teat between thumb and forefinger. If a drop of milk shows, all is well; if none has appeared after six hours, call the vet.

After a normal birth, the mother will have a discharge for several days. It should be bright red and odorless. If it has an odor and is dark in color, something may be wrong. Check with the vet.

As the mother nurses her young, she should be fed much the same diet as when she was pregnant, with plenty of milk and vitamin supplements. After three weeks, start decreasing the number of feedings but maintain the quantity. From six to eight weeks after birth she should be back to her normal feedings with, perhaps, vitamin supplements. While she's nursing her babies, keep her food and water bowls close by the nest. Also, her litter box.

Within ten days, the kittens' eyes will open. Mother will start their toilet training. You make sure their bellies are round and full. For the first four or five weeks, the mother's milk will be all the nourishment they need, though they will lap some water. Just in case there are more kits in the litter than the mother has teats, here is a good formula: boil a cup of homogenized milk, mix it with a couple of teaspoons of Karo syrup, an egg yolk, and a pinch of salt. Use a doll's

Siamese kittens are born all white. These five-week-old kittens are just beginning to show their points. The blue color of the eyes is so light that it appears clear in this photo. The red you see is actually the blood behind the eyes.

Mother and daughter are both shaded silver Persians, showing genetics applied practically. While the kitten is a trifle darker than the mother, the shading will lighten as it matures. When the kitten is full grown it will be almost indistinguishable from the mother.

These white Persian kittens are only six weeks old. Their hair will lengthen gradually as they mature.

nursing bottle. Put two or three teaspoons of the formula in the sterilized bottle; it should have a temperature of about 102°F. Serve frequently.

When the kittens are about a month old, clip their toenails, or, in play, they may scratch their mother's abdomen, or one another's eyes.

From their fifth to eighth weeks, they'll start on a weaning diet. Their sharp white teeth will appear and they'll then be able to tackle something stronger than milk. Give each a tablespoonful of raw scraped beef—warmed, of course— every few hours. Strained baby-food beef (Beechnut or Swifts) can be substituted. Alternate this with milk or the above-described formula. Some people do use precooked baby cereal (Pablum) at this time but I prefer the raw beef. The kits need a meat diet to build their stamina.

Gradually increase the solid foods. Meat, egg yolk and milk, possibly Pablum, or any cooked cereal, will make a good meal. Add cod-liver oil or commercially prepared vitamins to be sure they're getting all the nutrition they need. By the time the kittens are eight weeks old, they'll be weaned and ready for a diet that includes such delicacies as liver or boneless fish.

Mother cats do not always wean their kittens: they allow them to suckle even when there is no milk. Watch this. The kittens should be completely weaned by the time they are two months old. Start separating them gradually from their mother before they reach this age. By now they should also have had their temporary inoculations for Infectious Enteritis, and any other vaccinations that your veterinarian suggests.

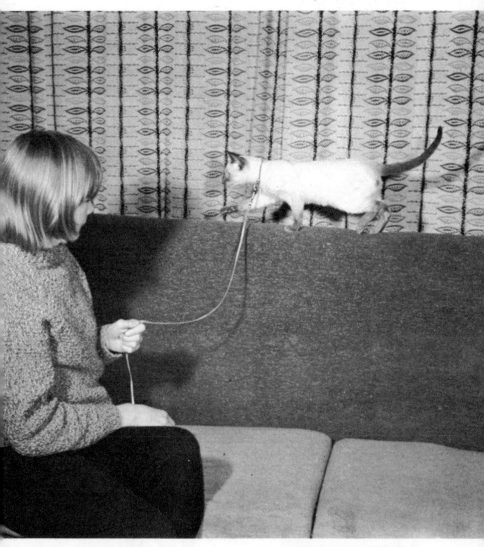

Train your Siamese to follow a lead. The first lessons should be given in the home where there are fewer distractions.

SI MERRILL

An infant Lion. At this age they are most appealing.